looking at art

1

FACES

Grolier Educational

SHERMAN TURNPIKE, DANBURY, CONNECTICUT 06816

Grolier Educational
Grolier Publishing Company, Inc.

Grolier Educational Staff
Joseph Tessitore, *Senior Vice President, Sales and Marketing*
Robert B. Hall, *Senior Vice President, Sales*
Beverly A. Balaz, *Vice President, Marketing*
A. Joseph Hollander, *Vice President and Publisher, School and Library Reference*
Molly Stratton, *Editor, School and Library Reference*

This edition first published 1996 by Grolier Educational, Danbury, Connecticut 06816.
Copyright © 1996 Marshall Cavendish Limited.

ISBN 0-7172-7595-7 (set)
ISBN 0-7172 7596-5 (volume)

Cataloging information can be obtained directly from Grolier Educational.

Marshall Cavendish Limited
Editorial staff
Series Consultant: Anthea Peppin,
Senior Education Officer, National Gallery, London
Series Editor: Tim Cooke
Editor: Sarah Halliwell
Senior Designer: Wayne Humphries
Picture Rights Coordinators: Vimu Patel, Sophie Mortimer
Text: Ian Chilvers
Index: Susan Dawson
Printed in Malaysia

Contents

Early & Renaissance Art

From the earliest times, artists have recorded what people looked like, in paintings, sculpture, and masks. How artists portrayed their subjects, from rulers to religious figures, could influence how others saw those people.

Portraits were very popular in Greek and Roman art. While very few paintings have survived from those ancient times, many sculptures have. Because the stone they were made from has lasted so well, these 2,000-year-old sculptures show us what such famous personalities as Alexander the Great and Julius Caesar probably looked like.

After the Emperor Constantine made Christianity the official religion of the Roman empire early in the fourth century, art became devoted almost exclusively to religious subjects. Even pictures or statues of the emperor himself became generalized images. Rather than show what his face was really like, artists tried to make him look more powerful. They gave him large, strong features—a long nose, round eyes, and a square chin—to make him look as they thought an emperor should.

Faces from the Bible

The faces that appeared in religious art were treated in a similar way. No one knew what Jesus or anyone else in the Bible really looked like. So

Emperor Constantine: Roman statue
This massive fourth-century statue—the head is 8 feet high—has large eyes to make the Roman emperor look more imposing.

artists imagined how religious figures might have looked. Over the years, these images became established in people's minds, so later painters simply repeated them. In early Christian art Jesus was usually shown without a beard and with short curly hair. Later, however, he was depicted with a beard and long flowing hair.

During the Middle Ages—the period from around the fifth century to the 15th—artists rarely painted realistic portraits. But the intellectual movement called the Renaissance encouraged artists to look more closely at all aspects of the world. From the 15th century, portraiture again became an important branch of art.

King Henry VIII:
Hans Holbein the Younger
Holbein shows the king's status by painting his chains and buttons in real gold.

Portraits of power

At first, only the most powerful people had their portraits painted. Wealthy people often paid to be included in religious paintings, to show how pious they were. Even when portraits were good likenesses, they more often concentrated on showing an individual's status in life rather than their personality.

A ruler, for example, wanted the subjects who saw his or her portrait to think them dignified and worthy of authority, even frightening. He or she would show off their wealth and power by being painted wearing elaborate costumes and expensive jewels.

The art of portraiture soon spread down the social scale. Anyone who could afford it, such as wealthy merchants or traders, could have their picture painted.

Portraits became varied and more individual, reflecting the wider selection of people that artists were now painting and their different roles in life. At the same time, painters of religious subjects made Jesus and the saints look more like real people than perfect, idealized visions.

5

The Betrayal of Christ

by Giotto (about 1266–1337)

The *Betrayal of Christ* is one of a series of scenes from the life of Jesus that Giotto painted in a small chapel in the northern Italian town of Padua in about 1305. One of Jesus's followers, Judas Iscariot, betrayed him to the Romans for 30 pieces of silver. He kissed Jesus as a sign to the soldiers that this was the man they should arrest.

Can you tell which of the central figures is Jesus, and which his betrayer? Giotto makes Jesus the tallest person in the painting and gives him a halo. If you look carefully you can see how the artist also contrasts Jesus's noble head—calm and unflinching amid the turmoil—with the treacherous face of Judas, who looks almost like an animal.

To the left, Giotto captures the emotion of the moment. One of Jesus's disciples, Saint Peter, is attacking Malchus, the servant of the High Priest. In his rage, the disciple cuts off Malchus's ear with a knife.

This is a fresco, a wall painting where the color was applied onto plaster that was still wet, creating a very permanent picture. Giotto worked on different patches at a time, because the plaster dried quickly.

Before Giotto, painted figures often lacked any sense of being real. Giotto not only depicted religious characters that looked more solid and three-dimensional than those of earlier artists, but also gave them the expressions and gestures of real people.

Giotto illustrated religious scenes that had been painted by other artists many times before. But he went straight to the heart of biblical stories and made them come alive.

Man in a Red Turban

by Jan van Eyck (about 1385–1441)

No one knows for sure who this sharp-eyed man is. The portrait is more than 500 years old—can you see the cracks in the paint caused by aging? In that time all records of its subject have been lost. But it is possible that this painting is a self-portrait of the artist.

Jan van Eyck lived in the city of Bruges, in the part of Europe that is now called Belgium. In van Eyck's time the region was known as Flanders, and the people who lived there Flemish or Netherlandish. It was a small but very prosperous region. International trade and finance made many of its people wealthy, and these citizens provided painters such as van Eyck with clients for their portraits.

Van Eyck was the most famous Flemish painter of his age. Among his important clients were the Duke of Burgundy, who was the ruler of Flanders, and the Church.

Van Eyck was very skilled at the technique of oil painting, which is still used today. Earlier artists had used a paint called tempera, which was mixed with the whites or yolks of eggs and was difficult to blend. With oil paint, artists could create finer detail and richer and more varied colors.

Van Eyck explored the possibilities of the medium. This portrait shows how he used it to capture different textures as well as colors. Look at the vibrant color of the complicated folds of the man's turban, for example. The striking blood-red stands out against the dark background. Can you see how the artist even shows the stubble on the man's chin?

Federigo da Montefeltro

by Piero della Francesca (about 1415/20–1492)

The man with the calm, strong, broken-nosed profile is called Federigo da Montefeltro. Federigo was duke of Urbino, a city-state in northern Italy, and ruled the territory around it. In the 15th century, Italy was not a single country. It was made up of different states, each with its own ruler, such as Federigo, or family of rulers.

Although Urbino was not one of the most powerful states in the country, it was an outstanding center of the arts. Federigo was a highly cultured man. His palace in Urbino is one of the most beautiful buildings of the Renaissance, and he employed some of the finest artists to decorate it.

The greatest artist to work for Federigo was Piero della Francesca, who painted this portrait as one of a pair—the other shows the duke's wife. Artists sometimes painted portraits showing the face sideways, or in profile. But there was a special reason why Piero depicted the duke like this.

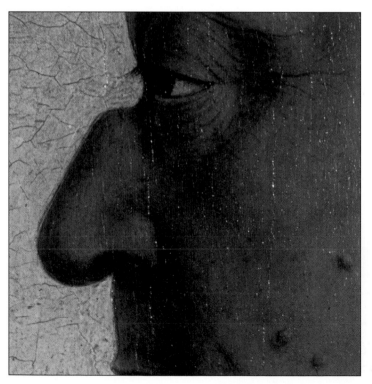

Federigo was a good soldier, which was very important as the Italian states often went to war with each other. Before going into battle, noblemen took part in tournaments to practice their military skills. In one of these, Federigo was so badly injured he lost his right eye.

By showing him from the left, Piero avoided the scarred side of his face. But you can't miss Federigo's misshapen nose. It was broken at the same time he lost his eye. How do you think it makes Federigo look? Funny? Or dignified because of the way he got his wound?

Christ Mocked

by Hieronymus Bosch (about 1450–1516)

Look at the sad, suffering face of Jesus at the center of this painting. How different it is from the vicious faces of the mob who mock him as he goes to his execution. Jesus carries the cross on which he will be crucified. In the top and bottom corners on the right are the two thieves who were crucified with him. Nearly everyone else is jeering at the condemned men.

Bosch's painting consists almost entirely of heads in close-up. This gives a vivid feeling of being carried along in a crowd, pressed up to the next person. But the artist has sympathy only with Jesus. Look at some of the people around him. Do

you think they look real or like cartoon characters out of a comic book? Why do you think that Bosch might have portrayed them in such a cruel way?

Can you see the only woman in the painting? She turns away from the scene in sorrow. According to legends that became attached to this Bible story, this is Saint Veronica. She wiped Jesus's brow with a cloth on which an image of his face then miraculously appeared.

On the back of this picture, Bosch painted the baby Jesus learning to walk. This was a reminder that Christ's journey to the Crucifixion began with his very first steps.

The Seventeenth & Eighteenth Centuries

By the 17th century, virtually anyone who had achieved some success in any walk of life—kings and princes, military leaders, clergymen, merchants, and traders—wanted a likeness painted.

Biblical and mythological figures no longer dominated art. There was little call for religious paintings in countries such as Holland, which had given up the Roman Catholic faith during the Reformation, when the Protestant religion had emerged.

Before photographs, portraits acted as a symbol of success. They were also a way in which someone could make sure that their name lived on after their death. Group portraits were a way of commemorating the work or achievement of a particular team of people.

Natural portraits

People naturally tried to look their best when they had their portrait painted, and usually posed in a dignified, formal way. However, some artists, such as the Flemish painter Frans Hals, realized that they could make people look more "alive" by showing them doing something natural—perhaps smiling or turning their head, or looking up from a book.

This kind of portraiture became very popular. The greatest painter of Holland, Rembrandt (*see page 17*), painted group portraits in a new way, making them more natural and informal. Just as revolutionary were his perceptive portraits—particularly those of his own face through the years, weathered by time.

Raising the status of portraits

In the 18th century formal portraits became popular again. A successful portraitist could become rich and famous. Yet the art of portraiture still did not have the same status as what was known as "history painting." This term meant the illustration of epic scenes from religion, mythology, and history. People believed it to be the most difficult and intellectually demanding type of painting. Therefore they rated it as being more important than other categories of art such as landscape and portraiture.

Inspiration from the past

Some artists, like Joshua Reynolds (*see page 19*), tried to make their portraits more like history paintings. They arranged their subjects in poses based on statues from ancient Greece or

Rome, or on the masterpieces of Renaissance painting. Artists still tried to capture a person's likeness, but in a way that looked historical.

The Laughing Cavalier: Frans Hals
Hals's portrait of a smiling, confident gentleman is one of the most famous images in the history of art.

The Guild of Drapers

by Rembrandt van Rijn (1606–1669)

The six men who look out at us with such penetrating expressions were responsible for making sure that all the cloth sold in 17th-century Amsterdam was of high quality. This was an important job. Amsterdam, the capital of Holland, was a thriving center of international trade, and it was essential to maintain high commercial standards.

A group of businessmen might sound like a dull subject for a painting, but Rembrandt has painted these soberly dressed men with immense dignity. Imagine you are a merchant or banker in the 17th century, and you have never met these men. Would this picture make you feel confident that the business affairs of Amsterdam were in safe hands?

Rembrandt worked in the country that we now call the Netherlands or Holland. In his time it was known as the Republic of the United Netherlands, or the Dutch Republic for short. Unlike most European countries in the 17th century, it was not ruled by a king or queen or dominated by rich aristocrats. The Dutch had fought hard for freedom from Spain, and their country was more like a modern democracy than any other nation. In other countries, only the rich could afford paintings, but in Holland fairly ordinary people bought them.

The Dutch wanted not only individual portraits but also pictures showing groups of real people at work or play. The sitters would usually pay to be included in such a painting. When people were proud of their success in their job they liked to have a record to commemorate their achievements, just like a photograph being taken today.

Rembrandt painted several group portraits. This one, painted in 1661, was the last. Many group portraits by earlier painters look very stiff, with the figures set out in rows so that they could all be recognized. But Rembrandt arranged his figures so that they look completely natural, as if we have interrupted them in the middle of their everyday business.

Look at the different expressions on the faces of these men. One looks as if he is in the middle of explaining something, his hand upturned on the open pages of a book. X-rays of this painting show that Rembrandt experimented with the positioning of the figures. Think how difficult it would be to arrange six figures round a table so that you could see all their faces but the scene still looked natural.

Garrick Between Tragedy & Comedy

by Joshua Reynolds (1723–1792)

David Garrick was the most famous English actor of the 18th century. Like celebrities today, he was very skillful at publicizing himself. He encouraged artists to paint his portrait. A portrait, however, took a long time and resulted in only one picture, which would not be seen by many people. So engravers made black-and-white copies of portraits, which could be printed in larger numbers. Garrick's admirers could buy these engravings in the same way that some movie fans today collect photographs of their favorite Hollywood stars.

This is one of the most original portraits of Garrick. Instead of a simple likeness, the artist, Joshua Reynolds, has painted an allegory— a scene with symbolic meaning. It is a version of a popular artists' subject from Greek myth known as "The Choice of Hercules." In the story the hero Hercules was forced to choose between two women. One represented a life of virtue and hard work, the other a life of ease and pleasure.

Reynolds adapts the theme and shows Garrick standing between two women who represent the two sides of the actor's art—Tragedy and Comedy. Which do you think is which? The woman on the right looks forbidding; the girl on the left is smiling invitingly. What choice do you think the actor is making? In the myth, Hercules chooses a life of virtue, represented by a stern-looking woman. But in this picture, Garrick seems to be choosing Comedy. He looks at Tragedy with a half-hearted smile of apology.

Do you think Garrick liked having his picture painted? He and Reynolds were good friends. Perhaps they enjoyed working together.

Death of Marat

by Jacques-Louis David (1748–1825)

"July 13, 1793. Marie Anne Charlotte Corday to Citizen Marat. My unhappiness is sufficient reason to entitle me to your kindness."

The artist David was a supporter of the Revolution and an admirer of Marat. He did not mean his picture to be a realistic depiction of the murder. Instead, he wanted to create an image of Marat as a martyr to his beliefs—an image by which Marat would be remembered as a hero. David concentrates the essential elements of the story into a very simple scene. Marat's face is serene. He looks like a martyred saint.

The man who slumps stabbed to death in his bath is Jean-Paul Marat. He was one of the leaders of the French Revolution, which in 1789 deposed the king and set up a republican government. The revolution was bloody, and Marat became one of its many victims.

Marat had a skin disease and used to spend a lot of time taking soothing baths. People even visited him while he was in the bathtub. On July 13, 1793, one of his visitors was a young woman called Charlotte Corday, a supporter of the monarchy. She stabbed Marat to death. Can you see the knife she used? The dead man clutches the letter his murderer wrote to get in to see him. The French reads:

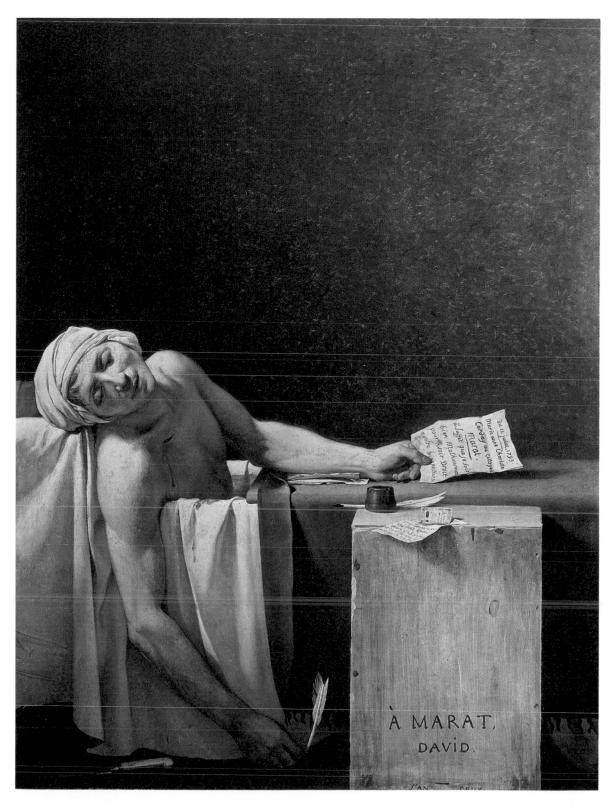

The Nineteenth Century

During the 19th century, artists tried new ways of painting new subjects. Rather than just painting people who paid them, some artists painted ordinary people who could never have afforded to pay for a portrait.

Throughout the 19th century one city dominated the development of art. The French capital, Paris, was the most important cultural center in the world. French painters were usually the leaders in new ideas.

The most revolutionary and influential art movement of the century was Impressionism, which began in Paris in the 1860s. Impressionist painters tried to convey a vivid feeling of the life going on around them. They depicted scenes of the everyday world that had not previously been used as subjects in art. They showed ordinary people enjoying themselves, dancing in clubs or drinking in cafés.

Pictures of the underclass

The industrialized world of the 19th century changed life for many people. In the great cities of Europe and the United States, an underclass emerged which was poor, lonely, desperate, and sometimes alcoholic. Earlier artists had used such people only as characters in larger paintings. Now the Impressionists treated them as subjects worth painting in their own right.

Absinthe: Edgar Degas
A working-class woman sits vacantly in a Paris café. This painting takes its name from the strong alcohol she is drinking.

Painters such as Degas showed the sadness of life as well as its happiness.

This new range of subject matter meant that painters looked with a fresh eye at all types of faces from all levels of society. Some, such as Édouard Manet, carried sketchbooks around so that they could make drawings of interesting faces or scenes wherever they saw them. And many of the Impressionists used friends and relatives as models.

The camera: friend or enemy?

When photography was invented in the 1830s, cameras were slow and cumbersome. They soon became much quicker. People were amazed at the detail photographs could show. Can you imagine how realistic even a black-and-white photograph must have appeared if you had only ever seen paintings and drawings?

Some of the Impressionists took photographs to help them paint. Snapshots let them capture momentary gestures and expressions that would look stiff and false if a model posed for them. Although these painters regarded the camera as a friend, others, especially portraitists, saw it as an enemy. They thought it would put them out of business.

But they were wrong. Although photography was a wonderful invention, a painting could do things it could not. It could convey color—color photography did not become really practical until the 20th century. It could be any size. And, most importantly, it could flatter a subject but still convey a good likeness.

Nineteenth-century artists gained inspiration not only from everyday life around them, but also from distant parts of the world. They realized that the art of other peoples often had a freshness and vigor absent from the more sophisticated art of the West. Paul Gauguin was one of the first Western painters to be inspired by "primitive" art. He spent most of the last ten years of his life living and painting among the natives of Tahiti, a remote island in the Pacific Ocean.

Tahitian Girl with a Flower:
Paul Gauguin
In this powerful portrait, Gauguin expresses the dignity of the Tahitian people.

23

Louis Bertin

by Jean-Auguste-Dominique Ingres (1780–1867)

What sort of job do you think this powerful-looking man might have had? The way he sits makes him look like someone important. His eyes look shrewd and

a little calculating. But he also seems like a down-to-earth, no-nonsense man. In fact, Louis-François Bertin was a successful French businessman and the owner of an important political magazine.

Bertin was 66 years old when Ingres painted this portrait. The artist had difficulty deciding on a suitable pose for Monsieur Bertin's burly figure. Originally he intended to show him standing up. One day, however, he saw a friend seated like this and realized that it would be ideal for suggesting his subject's forceful personality.

Ingres shows Bertin leaning slightly forward with his hands on his knees. The man almost looms out of the picture, so that we sense what it must have felt like to sit opposite him. The effect is enhanced by the extremely sharp, almost photographic detail. It is hard to imagine a portrait better conveying a living, breathing person.

But this portrait is not as accurate as it seems. One of Ingres's early sketches for the painting shows Bertin with characterless, limp hair. The artist has subtly changed his subject's appearance to give him more impressive hair and make his image more striking.

Bar at the Folies-Bergère

by Édouard Manet (1832–1883)

The young woman gazing rather sadly out at you is a barmaid at the Folies-Bergère, a famous cabaret and vaudeville club in Paris. Small bars like this lined the walls of the room. The background of the painting is a long mirror. You can see the audience among a glitter of lights. Can you spot the legs of a trapeze artist? On the right is a customer standing exactly where we are—in front of the barmaid. Can you imagine yourself as this top-hatted gentleman? Did you notice that the barmaid's reflection is in the wrong place? It should be behind her.

Although the painting is set in a nightclub, its mood is serious. Manet goes behind the glamor of the cabaret and gives us a feeling of the long hours and poor pay that the woman has to endure to make a living. The model

for this woman was a real barmaid called Suzon. Although Manet sometimes used professional models, he preferred working with "ordinary" people. He came from a very respectable family and sometimes shocked his contemporaries by painting low-life subjects that were thought unsuitable for a gentleman.

Sakata Hangoro III

by Toshusai Sharaku (active 1794–1795)

This fearsome-looking character is an actor cast as a villain in a Japanese play. Japanese theater is very different from Western drama. During the 17th century, a style emerged called kabuki. Kabuki drama brings together melodrama, music, and mime. The actors wear elaborate costumes and move in a way that is like dancing rather than normal gestures. A kabuki performance is more of a spectacular ritual than the kind of play you are used to seeing.

By the late 18th century, when Sharaku produced this print, kabuki actors were huge stars in Japan. Only men appeared onstage—they played the women's roles, too. Artists created prints that advertised coming performances or celebrated great roles by showing actors in character. The portraits were like today's posters of movie stars and sold very well to audiences wanting souvenirs of a performance they had enjoyed.

It took several wooden blocks to make a color print like this. Each was cut to a specific shape and inked with a separate color. Then all the blocks were carefully printed in sequence on one sheet of paper to produce a multi-colored print. These prints began to reach Europe and the United States in about 1850. Their bold shapes and colors had a great influence on Western artists of the time.

Can you see how this actor's eyes are squinting and his mouth is twisted in an evil expression? Do you think he looks funny—or frightening? What sort of details would you use to make someone look like a criminal?

Kabuki actors used makeup to exaggerate their expressions, but Sharaku may have gone too far with this picture. His views of many kabuki stars were so exaggerated and unflattering that some people even thought he might be an actor himself, but in a different type of theater called no. In any case, the artist's work was not popular; his publisher soon stopped producing his prints.

Self-Portrait

by Vincent van Gogh (1853–1890)

Look closely at van Gogh's eyes in this self-portrait. Can you see how he has placed a patch of green paint in the corner of one eye to draw your attention to his steady gaze? What do you see in his look? Although the artist seems calm and composed, the strokes of green and orange paint also give him a haunted look, as though he were full of feelings he is trying to keep under control. Perhaps those emotions burst out in the disturbed swirling patterns of blue

and gray that make up the background and the man's jacket.

When van Gogh painted this picture in 1889, his emotions were in turmoil. Only six weeks before, he had suffered a terrible mental breakdown. Now he was living in an asylum close to his home in southern France. Although van Gogh himself was very poor, his brother Theo paid for the artist to have his own bedroom and a studio where he could paint.

While he was in the asylum, van Gogh painted two pictures of himself. In both of them, he portrays himself as dignified and strong, despite the misery that he must have felt. In this picture the chaotic background threatens to engulf him. But the artist's neat beard and buttoned shirt suggest that he is trying to control the anger and confusion raging within his head. Every part of the portrait is painted with great energy.

Do you think that this portrait looks "real?" It is certainly a good likeness. Anyone would have been able to recognize van Gogh after they had seen this picture. But the painting would also tell them things about the artist's inner thoughts and feelings that they might not be able to guess from simply meeting him.

At the Moulin Rouge

by Henri de Toulouse-Lautrec (1864–1901)

All the characters in this painting were real people. The artist himself appears in profile just behind the people seated at the table. Toulouse-Lautrec was a very short man, and he shows his sense of humor by placing himself next to a very tall man who was his cousin in real life. Among the other people in the picture is a famous French dancer known as *La Goulue*, or "the Glutton." She appears in many other paintings by Toulouse-Lautrec.

The artist and his friends are gathered at the Moulin Rouge—or "Red Mill"—a dance-hall that opened in Paris in 1889. The nightclub inspired several of Toulouse-Lautrec's paintings. Although he was born into an aristocratic family, he preferred to spend his life among nightclub performers and prostitutes. At the time, singers and dancers were often considered disreputable and shady.

Toulouse-Lautrec captured the seedy glamor of the world these people lived in more vividly than any other artist. The women wear heavy makeup and are flashily dressed. The men look world-weary and old before their time.

Alcohol often features in this world. Toulouse-Lautrec himself died when he was only 36 years old, worn out by constant drinking and wild living. In spite of his lifestyle, however, he was dedicated to art. He would start painting early in the morning even after he had spent a drunken night on the town.

The Twentieth Century

In the last century art has changed more fundamentally than at any other time in history. Artists turned away from traditional subjects—some rejected altogether the idea of painting recognizable pictures of things or people.

Many artists in the past had found new ways of looking at the world. But however much they used their imagination or altered the appearance of things, they usually started by looking at what they saw around them. Now, toward the end of the 19th century, artists began to look inward for their subjects. They wanted to explore the fears and fantasies that haunt the mind.

Portraits of the mind

To convey their concerns, some artists used distorted shapes and bold, unnatural colors. Others went further in trying to show their inner feelings. Because they wanted to express what they felt, some of them became known as "expressionists."

Eventually this approach led to the emergence of what people called abstract art. Abstract art was wholly new. It did not try to represent anything that lay in the world outside the artist. It used colors and shapes to express emotions by themselves.

Artists' interests in their thoughts and feelings paralleled the work of the famous Austrian psychologist Sigmund Freud. During the last decades of the 19th century, Freud pioneered the understanding of the workings of the subconscious mind.

Lessons from other cultures

Twentieth-century artists also went further than their predecessors in their admiration of so-called "primitive" art from Africa, Latin America, and Asia. Many artists were greatly influenced by it. Only a few 19th-century artists, such as Paul Gauguin, had been inspired by the boldness and vitality of such art. Now, in the early years of the 20th century, many of the leading artists such as Amedeo Modigliani (*see page 37*) and Pablo Picasso collected African masks.

These masks belonged to long traditions of tribal art. For centuries people had carved wooden faces, decorating them with precious stones or with grass or straw for hair. Often these masks played an important part in religious ceremonies. Unlike European portraits, they did not simply try to capture a likeness of a real person. In fact, they often tried to alter a person's appearance by exaggerating certain features and simplifying others.

A warrior, for example, might wear a mask with staring eyes and snarling teeth. Such an appearance would not only terrify an enemy—it would also make the warrior himself feel more courageous. Have you noticed that when you wear a Halloween mask it sometimes makes you feel as though you were a different person? Other tribal masks portrayed the features of different gods. By wearing them, people believed that they could become closer to their deities.

It was not only the style of art that changed in the 20th century. The world was altering so quickly and in so many ways that people began to question art's traditional role. This was especially so after the First World War ended in 1918. The millions of deaths led many people to think that Western civilization was utterly rotten. Picasso, one of the greatest artists of the century, described painting as "an instrument of war against brutality and darkness."

Some artists reacted by mocking the values and art of the past. The most influential of them was Marcel Duchamp (*see page 41*), a Frenchman who spent much of his life in America. Many subsequent artists followed him in treating art as a kind of elaborate game or joke. Others, such as George Grosz (*see page 39*), tried to use their art to confront the ills of the world.

African mask:
Baule people, Ivory Coast
This wooden mask illustrates the Baule ideal of feminine beauty.

Jeanne Hébuterne
by Amedeo Modigliani (1884–1920)

Jeanne Hébuterne was Modigliani's girlfriend. The artist painted this portrait soon after they met in 1917. They had one child together and were expecting another. But the couple's happiness soon turned to tragedy when Modigliani died, aged only 35. He suffered from tuberculosis, but alcohol hastened his death. The next day, the heart-broken Jeanne jumped from an upstairs window, killing herself and her unborn child.

Can you see any sign of this tragic future in the picture? Or is Jeanne like any other woman who is young

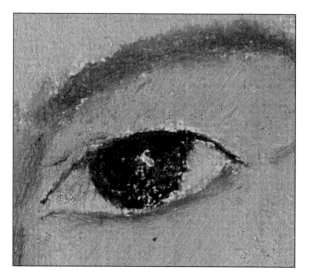

and in love? She certainly does not look worried or upset. In fact, she looks serene, almost happy—see how her mouth turns up in a slight smile.

Look at the woman's steady gaze and almond-shaped eyes. Now look back at the wooden mask on page 35. The elongated and simplified shape of Jeanne's face shows the influence of similar African masks.

Modigliani, an Italian who spent most of his career in Paris, was little known when he was alive, but is now very famous. More than anyone he represents the ideal of the "bohemian" genius who would suffer anything for his art. He lived in poverty and squalor, drinking endlessly, but all the while he was painting masterpieces.

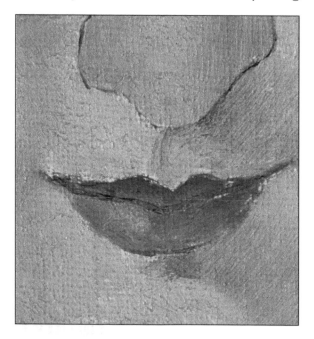

Pillars of Society

by George Grosz (1893–1959)

The hideous, cruel faces in this painting belong to members of Germany's ruling class in the 1920s. You can tell at once that the artist, George Grosz, did not like his subjects at all. Did you notice that one of the politicians in the foreground wears a chamber pot on his head? Another with a scarred face holds a glass of beer and waves a sword. Behind them a pompous priest gives his blessing as a building burns in the background. In the top corner of the painting soldiers go on the rampage. Can you see the blood stains on the sword one of them carries?

Grosz uses a technique often found in cartoons called caricature, in which people's features are exaggerated to make them look stupid, nasty, or laughable. Perhaps you have seen caricatures of today's politicians. But you will not see many that are as cruel to their subjects as these.

Grosz had good reason to be so cruel. Although he used cartoon techniques, his picture had a deadly serious purpose. When Grosz was alive, the political situation in Germany was increasingly chaotic and violent. The country was recovering from the effects of losing the First World War. In punishment for their aggression, the victors ordered the Germans to pay what was really a huge fine, called reparations. The country was nearly bankrupt. Poverty and unemployment increased.

Many Germans thought that only a ruthlessly strong government could lead Germany back to prosperity. Eventually this strong government came from Adolf Hitler, leader of the National Socialist party, called the Nazis. Can you see the symbol like a broken cross on the necktie of the man in the front of the painting? It is the swastika, the emblem of the Nazis.

The Nazis were aggressive and intolerant of opposition. They believed that only white Germans, or Aryans, were good and wanted to kill all Jews. This led to oppression, mass murder, and, when Germany invaded other countries, another world war, which Germany lost.

George Grosz believed he should use his art to point out what was wrong with the society in which he lived. He hated war and blind patriotism, and he was furious that rich people could live in style while poor people starved. He left Germany and settled in America just before Hitler came to power. If he had not done so, he would probably have been executed.

L.H.O.O.Q.

by Marcel Duchamp (1887–1968)

The *Mona Lisa* is the best-known face in the history of art. Leonardo da Vinci's famous portrait, painted more than 450 years ago, remains one of the most popular pictures ever painted. But look again at this woman's face. Did you notice the mustache and beard? In 1919 the French artist Marcel Duchamp took a pencil and drew them onto a postcard of Leonardo's picture.

Duchamp wanted to speak out against the seriousness of the art world. He belonged to a group of artists called the Dadaists who came together during the First World War and created works that seemed absurd or illogical, and often deliberately shocking. It was their way of expressing their disgust at the society that had created the war.

Some Dadaists even used violence to make their point. The German artist Max Ernst, for example, provided axes for visitors to an exhibit to smash the works on show. But Duchamp was more whimsical and humorous. As well as the mustache and beard, he added an inscription to the *Mona Lisa*—"L.H.O.O.Q."—which is a dirty joke in French.

To make his point, Duchamp used one of the most famous paintings in the world as the basis for his joke. For centuries, people have thought that the *Mona Lisa* was one of the greatest paintings of the long period of artistic achievement called the Renaissance. Can you see how natural the colors look? When Leonardo painted the portrait in about 1503, the subtle colors and the model's natural pose were new and surprising to his audience.

Do you know what the most famous part of this portrait is? It is the woman's expression. Look at the half-smile on her mouth. Do you think she looks happy or a little sad? Or perhaps you think that she looks mysterious, and you can't tell what she is thinking or feeling.

Duchamp took a painting that generations have respected as being a masterpiece and turned it into a joke. Look back at the other pictures in this book. Can you think of new titles that would give them a humorous new meaning?

Duchamp kept his joke going. Some years later he exhibited another postcard of the *Mona Lisa*. This time he had not altered Leonardo's picture at all, except that he had written on it the word "Rasée," which is French for "shaved"!

Izzy Ort's

by Edward Burra (1905–1973)

Look at the blank-eyed sailor who stares out from this painting of a bar in Boston during the 1950s. Does his face make you think that this would be a pleasant place to spend an evening? With his pug nose and blank expression, the man makes the bar seem unwelcoming. His face looks almost like a mask. Although everyone around him seems to be having a good time, his look gives the whole scene a feeling of menace and danger. Trouble could break out at any moment.

The English artist Edward Burra painted this picture on a trip to the United States. Like Impressionists such as Toulouse-Lautrec, he was fascinated by bars and nightclubs. Look back at Toulouse-Lautrec's painting of the Moulin Rouge (*see page 33*). Which of the two nightclubs do you think looks more inviting?

Can you see a handsome young man with a cigarette peering out between the two sailors in the foreground? This is a self-portrait of Burra. Just like Toulouse-Lautrec, he has included himself in the painting. He has the same empty eyes as the man in front of him.

Look at the woman on the right, however. She has used makeup to draw attention to her eyes. She wears heavy mascara on her lashes. Burra even paints tiny red veins in the corners of her eyes.

Why do you think Burra might be so interested in people's eyes? Perhaps it is because they are an artist's most important tool for seeing the world around him. Or perhaps they are the biggest clue to someone's personality.

GLOSSARY

abstract art: art that does not represent objects or people that can be recognized in the real world, but which expresses a thought, idea, or feeling through colors and shapes.

Baroque: a 17th and 18th century art movement that used elaborate and theatrical forms to appeal to the viewer's emotions.

classical art: the painting and sculpture of ancient Greece and Rome.

Cubism: a 20th-century painting style that showed the structure of things, often by displaying different views of the subject at the same time.

Expressionism: a style of art in which color and form are used to suggest moods and feelings rather than mimic what is seen.

fresco: a way of painting on walls in which color is applied straight onto a layer of wet plaster.

Futurism: an art movement that used new techniques to express the excitement and dynamism of the early 20th century.

Impressionism: a style of painting in which artists tried to capture the effects of light and the atmosphere of a scene.

Industrial Revolution: a period of rapid technological change in the early 19th century when many Western countries were transformed by new machines and industries.

medium: the material with which a work of art is created, such as pencil, oil, or watercolor.

Middle Ages: the period of European history that lasted from about the fifth to the 15th centuries.

naïve art: a name given to art produced by untrained artists who often do not use advanced techniques such as perspective.

naturalism: an approach to art in which everyday objects, places, and people are shown without trying to idealize their appearance.

oil paint: a type of paint that uses oils to bind together the color.

pastel: crayons made from chalk and powdered pigment, which smudge on paper.

perspective: a method of drawing used to create an illusion of depth in a flat picture, using lines that meet at a single spot on the horizon known as the "vanishing point."

portrait: a painting that gives a likeness of a person and often an insight into his or her personality.

primitivism: a type of art that uses the shapes and symbols of tribal cultures from, for example, Africa, South America, or Asia.

realism: an approach to art that sees even ugly and unhappy scenes as being suitable subjects for artists.

Reformation: a 16th-century religious movement that protested many of the ideas of the Catholic Church and established the Protestant faith.

Renaissance: the "rebirth" of classical ideas that began in 14th century Italy, lasted to the 17th century, and led to a flowering of the visual arts and literature.

Rococo: An art movement of the early 18th century that used a delicate, elegant, decorative style.

Romanticism: a 19th-century movement in art and literature that celebrated the exotic, passionate, and dangerous.

sketch: a rough or quick version of a picture, often produced as a trial-run for a more finished work.

still life: a drawing or painting of objects that cannot move by themselves, such as fruit and flowers.

Surrealism: a 20th-century art movement that combines odd images to express the irrational and subconscious world of dreams or fantasy.

technique: the way an artist uses his or her materials.

watercolor: a type of paint in which colors dissolve in water.

looking at art
SET INDEX

FURTHER READING

Cummings, Pat, ed. *Talking with Artists*. Bradbury, 1992.

Greenberg, Jan, and Jordan, Sandra. *The Painter's Eye: Learning to Look at Contemporary Art*. Delacorte, 1991.

Isaacson, Philip M. *A Short Walk Around the Pyramids & Through the World of Art*. Knopf, 1993.

Janson, H.W. *History of Art*. Harry N. Abrams, Inc., 1995.

Powell, Jillian. *Painting and Sculpture*. Steck-Vaughn, 1990.

Sills, Leslie. *Visions: Stories about Women Artists*. Albert Whitman, 1993.

Testa, Fulvio. *If You Take a Paintbrush: A Book of Colors*. Dial, 1983.

Waterford, Giles. *Faces*. Atheneum, 1982.

Woolf, Felicity. *Picture This: A First Introduction to Paintings*. Doubleday, 1990

Yenawine, Philip. *Colors*. Delacorte, 1991; *Lines*. Delacorte, 1991; *Shapes*. Delacorte, 1991.

Zadrzynska, Ewa. *The Girl with a Watering Can*. Chameleon, 1990.

PICTURE CREDITS